LOUIS AGASSIZ FUERTES
Painter of Birds

by James Je...

Louis Agassiz Fuertes Papers, 1892-1954. Collection Number 2662. Courtesy of the Division of Rare and Manuscript Collections, Cornell University Library.

HOUGHTON MIFFLIN   BOSTON

D1417382

Louis Agassiz Fuertes

Louis Agassiz Fuertes was born in 1874. He was an artist. He was also a naturalist. A naturalist is someone who studies nature. Naturalists want to conserve, or take care of, our natural resources.

Fuertes liked the drawings of birds by John James Audubon.

Louis loved birds when he was a little boy. He drew many pictures of them. His father showed him pictures of birds. John James Audubon drew those pictures. He was a naturalist too. He lived before Louis was born.

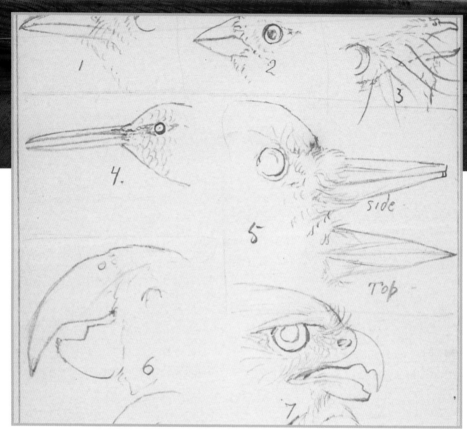

Fuertes's early drawings

Louis's father was from Puerto Rico. He was a teacher at a college. His father wanted Louis to go to college too. But Louis didn't do very well in college. Louis was not sad. He knew he wanted to paint birds for a living.

Fuertes stayed in houses like these while he was in Alaska.

In college Louis met another artist and learned more about painting from him. Then, Louis went to Alaska. He studied and drew birds. He looked for birds that were new to him. Louis made notes about the new birds that he drew.

A painting of mallard ducks by Fuertes

Louis was always looking for new birds to paint. He often painted birds that were dead, but sometimes he studied birds that were still alive. He went to many places to learn more about birds. He taught others a lot about birds.

PRINCE— aug 4, 1902.   L.A.F

Fuertes used watercolors to paint this dog.

Louis Agassiz Fuertes Papers, 1892-1954. Collection Number 2662. Courtesy of the Division of Rare and Manuscript Collections, Cornell University Library.

Louis drew animals too. His drawings were put in a book for children. The book was about animals.

Louis Agassiz Fuertes drawing the background for one of his pictures

Louis Agassiz Fuertes Papers, 1892-1954. Collection Number 2662. Courtesy of the Division of Rare and Manuscript Collections, Cornell University Library.

Louis made his birds look real. He made sketches of over 400 different kinds of birds. He even made murals for a museum. He died in 1927. He was a famous painter of birds during his lifetime.